THE JUICING SECRET

In the same series

The Blender Book
Steaming!
The Fan Oven Book
Wicked Puddings

Uniform with this book

THE
JUICING
SECRET

Norma Miller

RIGHT WAY

Typeset in 10/11 pt by Letterpart Ltd., Reigate, Surrey.

Printed and bound in Great Britain by Cox & Wyman Ltd., Reading, Berkshire.

The *Right Way* series is published by Elliot Right Way Books, Brighton Road, Lower Kingswood, Tadworth, Surrey, KT20 6TD, U.K. For information about our company and the other books we publish, visit our web site at www.right-way.co.uk

CONTENTS

INTRODUCTION

Juicing is an adventure. Juices are stimulating, exciting, refreshing and healthy. I know that my own enthusiasm for juicing is shared by many people. I hope this book will provide some intriguing new ideas for experienced juicers, at the same time as it gives encouragement and advice to any reader drawn to experimenting with juicing for the first time.

The range of fruit and vegetables which can be, literally, pressed into service in the making of juices is immense. This diversity, and the unusual combinations to which it gives rise, are for me an essential part of the juicing experience.

This book will first introduce you to your juicing machine, showing you how it functions, and also will describe the two basic types of juicing machine. A chapter on the healthful vitamins and minerals to be found in juices is followed by some general advice. This covers the selection and preparation of fruit and vegetables to be used in juicing, and ways to gain maximum enjoyment from the pure juices you can create from them. A further chapter brings in some other ingredients which will turn your pure juices, remarkable enough in themselves, into some delicious speciality treats.

The emphasis throughout is on the pleasure to be had in juices as a healthy product, using fresh, varied and invigorating ingredients in simple or complex combinations. Juices can be prepared and served at any hour of the day in order to bestow vitality, refreshment and an undoubted sense of well-being.

I have myself gained great pleasure from all the juicing which has led to the appearance of these recipes. There is a real sense of expectation, followed by satisfaction, in the juicing of a previously untried variety of fruit or an unfamiliar vegetable, and the same goes for unlikely mixtures of fruit and vegetables. It is worth doing a little experimentation of your own, because it is surprising how often the results will be a success.

Above all, your juicing machine is terrific fun. The secret of juicing is in the all-round enjoyment, so enjoy juicing.

Acknowledgements
I would like to thank Waring for the loan of the Kitchen Classics by Waring juice extractor. A juicing machine which could cope with the huge quantities of fruit and vegetables which I juiced to test these recipes. It was indispensable.

For stockists of Kitchen Classics by Waring please telephone 020 8232 1800.

1

THE JUICER: THE ESSENTIAL PIECE OF EQUIPMENT

It is possible to juice by hand but this is very time-consuming and messy, so the solution is to use an electric version.

This basically consists of a powerful motor base on which sits a covered bowl holding a basket and blade. Once you switch the machine on, the motor will rev into action. You then slowly feed the prepared fruit and vegetables through a feeder tube in the lid using a pusher. You simply switch the machine off when you want it to stop.

Juicing takes a matter of minutes, a similar time for fruit and vegetables. Once you have fed the fruit and vegetables into the machine, juice will immediately begin to flow through the spout (remember to put a glass under the spout). Allow the machine to run for one to three minutes for maximum extraction, but stop when the juice doesn't flow; don't over juice. All juicers are slightly different so follow the manufacturer's guidelines in the instruction booklet.

What to consider before purchase
- What is your budget? There are many models on the market covering a wide price band.

- Will you get the juicing bug? If so, one of the more powerful deluxe professional models capable of coping with frequent use may be more suitable.

- The deluxe models often have the option of a citrus juicer attachment. This is an electric version of a manual press juicer. It is ideal if you just want a small amount of

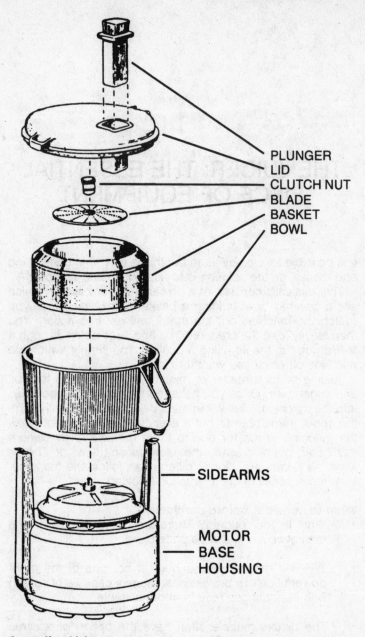

PLUNGER
LID
CLUTCH NUT
BLADE
BASKET
BOWL

SIDEARMS

MOTOR
BASE
HOUSING

A centrifugal juicer.
(Illustration courtesy of New Classics Ltd, Hatfield.)

juice and can be used with halved citrus fruit, such as lemons, limes, oranges or grapefruits. The attachment fits into the bowl of the juicer and will only slowly turn when pressure is applied to the upturned fruit.

- If you are a real beginner at juicing then choose a basic cheaper version.

- Look at all the machines available, some stores have regular demonstrations of electrical kitchen equipment.

- Early morning is a popular time for using a juicer so the noise levels of the machine will be very important.

- Does the machine vibrate and move across the work surface?

- Juicers with smaller motors will not extract as much juice as those more powerful models.

- Most are easy to assemble and maintain. But remember, juicing is a sticky business and the machine will need washing after every use. I think you have to include this in the ritual of juicing.

What types of juicers are available?
For domestic use there are basically two types of juicer: a centrifugal juicer and a masticating juicer.

Centrifugal juicer
This is the most widely used juicer. The prepared fruit and vegetables are fed, with the help of a plunger, through the lid of the juicer into a plastic or stainless steel basket which then spins at high speed. The juice is separated from the pulp and flows out into a glass or jug.

Some machines use disposable wide strips of filter paper in the bowl. This makes it easier to remove the pulp and therefore the machine is easier to clean.

Masticating juicer
The prepared fruit and vegetables are fed into the juicer. They are then ground into a paste before being spun round at high speed to extract the juice through a screen in the base of the juicer.

Notes

- The quantities of juice produced from fruit and vegetables will vary due to: the type of machine used; the time of year (fruit will give more juice in the summer) and the type of fruit and vegetable used (cucumbers, tomatoes and melons will give 2-3 glasses or even more, whilst beetroot or cabbage will give a much smaller amount).

- When juicing, alternate pushing hard and soft fruit through the machine. This will stop the machine vibrating and becoming clogged.

- The pulp left behind in the machine does have a use. Use a little on your cereal or replace some of the dried fruit in muffins, fruit cakes and tea breads. Or add to your compost heap.

2

THE HEALTH BENEFITS
OF JUICING

Do you always have your five portions of fruit and vegetables every day?
Most of us would say that we are too busy to eat five portions of fruit and vegetables every day, but research shows that this helps to protect us against heart disease and cancer. We know that fruit and vegetables are good for us, and yet we still forget to eat them. The good news is that a glass of fruit or vegetable juice counts as one of the daily portions and is the perfect way to start the day, or to ease into a relaxing evening.

As part of a healthy diet, fruit and vegetables contain over a hundred vitamins, minerals and other nutrients which help to keep our bodies healthy.

Here are some guidelines.

- If you are new to juices it is recommended that you start by drinking them in small quantities at first, and then steadily increase the quantities as you become used to them.

- It is best to drink your juices as soon as they are made as the nutritional value starts to deteriorate with any delay. Once exposed to the air many vitamins will oxidise and the health benefits are reduced.

- Juices in your diet will provide some of the following nutrients.

Antioxidants
Antioxidants play a role in the body's natural defence mechanisms.

Beta-carotene
Is part of the carotenoids group and can be split in the body to be turned into **Vitamin A**. It may help to boost the immune system and so is protection against the risk of heart disease and cancers.

Found in yellow, orange, red and dark green fruit and vegetables.

Calcium
Essential for bone development.

Found in green vegetables, milk, yoghurt and tofu.

Carotenoids
These are part of a group of antioxidants which protect the body's cells and help to prevent degenerative diseases including cancer and cardiovascular problems.

Found in yellow, orange, red and dark green fruit and vegetables.

Chlorophyll
This is the green colouring in plants and gives the body energy.

Flavonoids
These are part of a group of antioxidants which help to prevent degenerative diseases including cancer and cardio-vascular problems.

Folic acid
Important for the function of blood cells.

Found in beetroot, green leafy vegetables and citrus fruit.

Iron
Important for the function of red blood cells.

Found in dark green leafy vegetables.

Magnesium
Important for growth and repair of the body.

Found in soya 'milk', peas, nuts and sesame seeds.

Natural sugars
Fructose is the natural sugar found in some fruit and vegetables. This natural sweetness means that you don't need to sweeten juices with extra sugar.

Phosphorus
Helps with the growth of bones and teeth.
    Found in cabbage, potato, oranges, cherries and currants.

Potassium
Important for cell function.
    Found in many vegetables and fruit including bananas.

Protein
Essential for the growth of the body and for energy.
    Found in most foods.

Vitamin B complex
Helps the maintenance of the nervous system.
    Found in vegetables, apples, bananas and apricots.

Vitamin C
Helps the immune system and is an antioxidant.
    Found in green vegetables, tomatoes, berries, currants, citrus fruit, kiwi fruit and pineapples.

Vitamin E
An antioxidant that helps rid the body of free radicals.
    Found in broccoli, spinach, sweet potatoes, watercress and wheatgerm.

Vitamin K
Necessary for the normal clotting of the blood.
    Found in spinach, cabbage, cauliflower and peas.

Zinc
Helps with the healing of wounds.
    Found in leafy vegetables.

3

VEGETABLE KNOW-HOW

The popularity of juicing and the search for new ingredients have raised the profile of vegetables, in all their profuse variety, as a contrast to the more familiar fruit juices. Vegetable juices have their own distinctive range of flavours, with some showing unexpected sweetness (carrots being a good example of this), whereas the hallmark of many is their earthy, herbal vigour. These robust and evocative flavours are a voyage of discovery.

There really aren't any vegetables which can't be juiced. Just try your favourites, even potatoes, and see if you like the flavours. However, it is difficult to juice an avocado; it's much better to mash a ripe avocado with a fork or potato masher or to use an electric wand-style mixer.

For the best possible results with juicing vegetables, here are some tips to bear in mind.

- For juicing, it is important to select only vegetables of the very finest quality. Buy organic vegetables if you can.

- Make sure that the vegetables you choose for juicing are in perfect condition. Do not, on any account, use damaged or shrivelled vegetables – the results will be disappointing.

- Remember to wash vegetables thoroughly before you start to prepare them for juicing. This will remove any soil or impurities still adhering to them.

- Clean root vegetables by scrubbing them firmly with a nail brush reserved for this purpose.

- When preparing the vegetables, cut or tear them (according to the recipe) into manageable pieces so that the chunks can be pushed easily into the feed tube of the juicing machine.

- Juice the vegetables as soon as they have been prepared.

- Always drink vegetable juices cold. They can be chilled, or you can add crushed ice or ice cubes.

- Juices from a juicing machine are naturally very concentrated and usually need to be diluted. If your preference is for longer drinks, which many people find more refreshing, dilute juices with the desired quantity of water.

Roots/Bulbs often with their leaves
Beetroots, carrots, celeriac, fennel, radishes, mooli (white radishes), onions, parsnips, sweet potatoes, turnips.
  2 medium-sized beetroots give approximately 150ml/¼ pint of juice.
  2 medium-sized carrots give approximately 150ml/¼ pint of juice.
  Preparation: Scrub root vegetables with a nail brush and trim off the roots. Cut both the root and top off carrots as this is where pesticides will congregate. Cut into manageable sizes.

Stems/Stalks
Asparagus, broccoli, cauliflower, celery, spring onions.
  2 celery stalks give approximately 4 tablespoons of juice.
  Preparation: If necessary, trim any roots, leave whole or roughly chop.

Fruiting vegetables

Courgettes, cucumber, French beans, runner beans, peas, peppers, squash, tomatoes.

2 courgettes give approximately 150ml/¼ pint of juice.

1 cucumber gives approximately 300ml/½ pint of juice.

1 red pepper gives approximately 75ml/2½ fl oz of juice.

115g/4 oz French beans give approximately 3-4 table-spoons of juice.

Preparation: Remove the stalks from the tomatoes and halve if large. Trim both ends of the beans, cucumbers and courgettes. Halve peppers, remove the stalk and the seeds. Prepare squashes as you would a melon.

Leaves

Chicory, dandelion leaves, all types of lettuce, kale, nettles, pak choi, spinach, Swiss chard, watercress.

3 leaves of kale or cabbage give approximately 4 tea-spoons of juice.

Preparation: Trim off any roots. I find it a help to twist and roll the leaves into tight balls. This enables the juice to be extracted more easily from the leaves, and prevents the juicing machine from becoming clogged.

Herbs and others

Lemon balm, basil, borage, chives, coriander, cress, lavender, mint, parsley, rocket, sage.

Alfalfa sprouts, chillies, garlic, ginger, horseradish, wheat-grass.

Give a small amount of juice but lots of flavour.

Preparation: Carefully remove any woody twigs and roll and twist the herbs into small bundles.

4

FRUIT KNOW-HOW

There is something perennially exciting and invigorating about a glass of pure juiced fruit. It is a true pleasure, which can give you a lift whenever you need it.

As with vegetables, there isn't really any fruit which can't be juiced. Just try your favourites and see if you like the flavours. However, it is very difficult to juice a banana; it's much better to mash a ripe banana with a fork or potato masher or to use an electric wand-style mixer. Also I think rhubarb makes a too acidic juice.

For the best possible results, here are some tips to bear in mind.

*   It is important to select for juicing only the very best quality fruit. Choose carefully from the varieties available to you; different types of apples, pears and oranges will produce juices with distinctive flavours. Buy organic fruit whenever you can.

*   Make sure that the fruit you use for juicing is in perfect condition. At all costs avoid bruised or damaged fruit.

- Many types of fruit will soften with age. Don't use over-ripe fruit. It is better to use firm, crisp fruit; not only is it fresher, but it will (perhaps surprisingly) provide you with more juice.

- Do remember to wash all fruit thoroughly before you start to prepare it for juicing. By this means, you will remove any impurities from the surface of the fruit.

- Fruit is sometimes given a waxy coating by a process designed to prolong storage. Apples, pears and citrus fruit can be treated in this way. It is better to use unwaxed fruit.

- If you suspect that the fruit you are intending to use for juicing has been waxed, you will first need to remove the waxed surface. For citrus fruit this means you should vigorously scrub each piece of fruit with a clean vegetable brush or nail brush kept for this purpose. For apples, pears and similar fruit the skin should be peeled so that it is completely removed.

- When preparing the fruit, cut or tear it (according to the recipe) into manageable pieces so that the chunks can be pushed easily into the feed tube of the juicing machine.

- Juice the fruit as soon as it has been prepared.

- Always drink fruit juices cold. They can be chilled, or you can add crushed ice or ice cubes.

- Juices from a juicing machine are naturally very concentrated. If your preference is for longer drinks, which many people find more refreshing, dilute juices with the desired quantity of water.

Berries, currants and other soft fruit
Blackberries, blackcurrants, blueberries, cranberries, black, red or green seedless grapes, raspberries, redcurrants, strawberries.
   115g/4 oz blackcurrants give approximately 100ml/3½ fl oz of juice.
   175g/6 oz black or green seedless grapes give approximately 150ml/¼ pint of juice.

115g/4 oz redcurrants give approximately 75ml/2½ fl oz of juice.

175g/6 oz strawberries give approximately 50ml/2 fl oz of juice.

Preparation: Carefully look through all the fruit and remove any woody or twiggy stalks. Pull off the green tops from strawberries. Grapes can be used with or without pips, but I prefer to use seedless varieties.

Citrus fruit

Grapefruits, limes, lemons, and oranges in all their varieties such as clementines, mandarins, satsumas and tangerines.

1 grapefruit gives approximately 150ml/¼ pint of juice.

1 lime gives approximately 1 tablespoon of juice.

1 lemon gives approximately 50ml/1 fl oz of juice.

2 oranges give approximately 150ml/¼ pint of juice.

Preparation: Only remove the thin outer peel from citrus fruit, leaving behind as much of the white pith as possible. The pith contains powerful antioxidants. Cut the fruit into manageable wedges.

Melons

Cantaloupe, galia, honeydew, ogen, and watermelon.

A quarter of a watermelon gives approximately 500ml/ 18 fl oz of juice.

Preparation: Cut melons into quarters or wedges and then scoop out and discard the seeds. Cut the flesh away from the skin and roughly chop.

Orchard fruit

Apples and pears.

2 apples give approximately 150ml/¼ pint of juice.

2 pears give approximately 200ml/7 fl oz of juice.

Preparation: Remove the stalks from the washed or peeled apples and pears then cut into wedges. There's no need to remove the core and pips.

Stone fruit

Apricots, cherries, lychees, nectarines, peaches, plums.

6 apricots give approximately 3 tablespoons of juice.

2 peaches give approximately 125ml/4 fl oz of juice.

6 plums give approximately 200ml/7 fl oz of juice.

Preparation: Remove any woody stalks from the washed fruit, cut them in half, remove the stones and slice the flesh.

Tropical fruit

Kiwi fruit, mangoes, guavas, persimmons, papaya, pineapples, passion fruit, pomegranates.

2 passion fruit give approximately 3 tablespoons of juice.

1 large pineapple gives approximately 500ml/18 fl oz of juice.

Preparation: The fruit in this section needs slightly different handling. Kiwi fruit, guavas and persimmons just need cutting into wedges. Slice passion fruit and pomegranates in half and scoop out the edible seeds. Peel the papaya, scoop out the seeds then slice the flesh away from the peel. With mangoes, peel away the skin and cut the flesh away from the stone. Slice both ends off a pineapple, cut away the thick skin and cut the flesh into manageable pieces.

Others

Surprisingly, some dried fruit, such as apricots or prunes, can be juiced. Soak in water for an hour and then juice as normal.

Soaked dried fruit gives a small amount of juice but lots of flavour.

Some fruit is only available for a very limited season so freeze for juicing another time and use from frozen.

5

JUICING EXTRAS

By juicing medleys of fruit and vegetables in almost infinite combinations you have a stunning variety of pure juices at your fingertips. But beyond this you can do even more with your juicing. By the addition of some stimulating and refreshing ingredients, you can transform your pure juice into a sparkling array of drinks and desserts, soups, smoothies, ices, punches and cocktails.

Here are some ideas for additional ingredients. Use your imagination to the full.

Dairy and non-dairy additions
Smoothies are juices which have been mixed with yoghurt, milk, cream or non-dairy 'milk' such as that made with soya.

There are several types of yoghurt available from full-fat, thick Greek, low fat, natural, bio, and frozen. Cows, goats, and sheep provide natural milk allowing you many permutations.

Alcoholic additions
A splash of something alcoholic does revive the spirits although it is clearly advisable to use alcohol in moderation.

In the recipes I've delved into the booze cupboard and used a little vodka, wine, dry vermouth, champagne, Cointreau, angostura bitters, Marsala, brandy and rum. But not all in the same recipe I hasten to add! Alcoholic additions are used to best effect when applied singly.

Non-alcoholic additions

Chilled still or sparking water and ice, whether crushed or in cubes, is essential. It is often necessary to dilute juices; in fact, vegetable juices can be quite powerful and are an acquired taste (and a taste worth acquiring).

I rather like the fragrant perfume a little elderflower water, orange blossom water or rosewater gives to apple, pear or orange juice.

For cocktails or punches there's a huge variety of non-alcoholic wines, or just add grape juice and sparkling water.

Toppings

Maybe they can't be classed as 'healthy' but sometimes you need to be a little self-indulgent, and it is nice to treat your family or friends to something a little naughty. Top a tall glass of juice or a smoothie with mini marshmallows, grated chocolate or crushed peanut brittle.

A healthier option would be a few walnut pieces, toasted cumin seeds, pecan nuts or a little wheatgerm.

Add a little spice with a dusting of ground nutmeg, cinnamon or black pepper.

Other flavourings

Many fruit juices rely on the natural sugars in the fruit to give sweetness.

For more acidic fruit you may prefer to sweeten juices with a little maple syrup or clear honey, but only add enough to taste.

A dash of Worcestershire sauce or balsamic vinegar will bring spice and flavour to savoury juices.

Coconut cream, the type you buy in a small carton or tin, will add a Thai or Caribbean flavour, delicious if you serve the juices at parties.

A glass of juice becomes an American-style 'float' when a scoop of good quality ice cream is floated on top.

Bananas

They are here in a section on their own because they are a necessary and exciting addition for some smoothies, but are very difficult to juice. A ripe banana when mashed will thicken a juice and add vital nutrients. Crush a ripe banana with a fork or potato masher.

Juices and frozen lollies
Fruit juices can quickly be turned into healthy, naturally sweet iced lollies. Pour your chosen juice into iced-lolly moulds or clean, small, plastic yoghurt pots plus small lolly sticks (use small wooden skewers if you can't find lolly sticks), and freeze until solid. See the recipe for Rainbow Lollies on page 122.

Granita
Granita is an Italian ice, a frozen mix of fruit juices or vegetable juices plus flavourings such as garlic or herbs, or ground cinnamon or ginger, which freezes to an icy mass and is scraped with a spoon into glasses. See the recipe for Plum and Cranberry Granita, page 118.

Soups
Soups, both hot and cold, are quickly made from fruit and vegetable juices plus a little spicing and a swirl of yoghurt or cream. Either heat in a pan or chill with ice cubes. See the recipes for Carrot and Orange Soup, page 99, or Chilled Orange and Strawberry Soup, page 123.

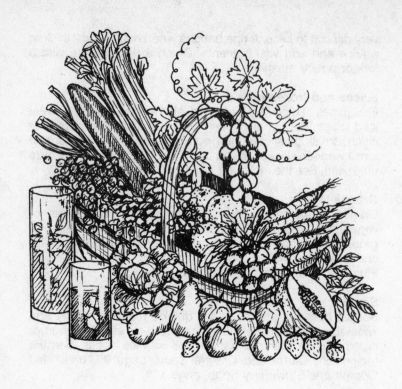

6

RECIPES: SAVOURY AND SWEET JUICES

Pepper, Orange and Beetroot

For a meal in a glass stir in some thick Greek yoghurt.

A source of vitamins B complex and C, flavonoids, calcium and folic acid, iron and potassium.

Serves 1-2

1 red pepper
4 oranges
2 green apples
2 small beetroots
Chilled still or sparkling water
Crushed ice or ice cubes

1. Halve the pepper, remove the stalk and scrape out the seeds. Cut the pepper into wedges.

2. Remove the outer peel from the oranges, leaving behind the white pith, and cut into wedges.

3. Remove the stalks from the apples and cut into wedges.

4. Roughly slice the beetroots.

5. Juice the pepper, oranges, apples and beetroots.

6. Pour the juice into tall glasses and if preferred dilute with water or ice.

7. Serve immediately.

Fennel, Apple and Ginger

Fennel and ginger are very calming and good for digestion.

A source of vitamin C, beta-carotene, flavonoids, iron and potassium.

Serves 1-2

4 green eating apples
1 fennel bulb
Small piece of root ginger
Chilled still or sparkling water
Crushed ice or ice cubes

1. Remove the stalks from the apples and cut into wedges.

2. Trim the base of the fennel and cut into wedges.

3. Juice the ginger, apples and fennel.

4. Pour the juice into tall glasses and if preferred dilute with water or ice.

5. Serve immediately.

Carrot and Orange Booster

A real energy booster, this is just the drink to start the day or when your energies are flagging.

A source of vitamins A, B complex and C, flavonoids, calcium, folic acid, iron, magnesium and potassium.

Serves 1-2

5 carrots
3 oranges
Small piece root ginger
Chilled still or sparkling water
Crushed ice or ice cubes

1. Scrub the carrots and remove both ends. Cut into chunks.

2. Remove the outer peel from the oranges, leaving behind the white pith, and cut into wedges.

3. Juice the ginger, carrots and oranges.

4. Pour the juice into tall glasses and if preferred dilute with water or ice.

5. Serve immediately.

Apple, Pepper and Pea

A surprise juice. Make in the summer when fresh sweet young peas are available, although frozen peas can be used to good effect.

A source of vitamins B complex and C, beta-carotene, folic acid, phosphorus and potassium.

Serves 1-2

3 green apples
1 green pepper
6 mint sprigs
175g/6 oz peas
Chilled still or sparkling water
Crushed ice or ice cubes

1. Remove the stalks from the apples and cut into wedges.

2. Halve the pepper, remove the stalk and scrape out the seeds. Cut the pepper into wedges.

3. Juice the mint sprigs, apples, pepper and peas.

4. Pour the juice into tall glasses and if preferred dilute with water or ice.

5. Serve immediately.

Carrot, Tomato and Cucumber Froth

The juice separates into layers with a thick froth on the surface.

A source of vitamins A, C and E, beta-carotene, folic acid, magnesium and potassium.

Serves 2

3 carrots
6 tomatoes
1 orange
½ cucumber
Chilled still or sparkling water
Crushed ice or ice cubes

1. Scrub the carrots and remove both ends. Cut into chunks.

2. Remove the stalks from the tomatoes and halve if large.

3. Remove the outer peel from the orange, leaving behind the white pith, and cut into wedges.

4. Trim the ends off the cucumber and cut into chunks.

5. Juice the carrots, tomatoes, orange and cucumber.

6. Pour the juice into tall glasses and if preferred dilute with water or ice.

7. Serve immediately.

Watercress, Fennel and Spinach

A revitalising juice with a peppery aniseed-like flavour.

A source of vitamins C and E, beta-carotene, calcium, folic acid and iron.

Serves 1-2

4 green eating apples
1 fennel bulb
1 bunch watercress
1 handful spinach leaves
Chilled still or sparkling water
Crushed ice or ice cubes

1.   Remove the stalks from the apples and cut into wedges.

2.   Trim the base of the fennel and cut into wedges.

3.   Juice the watercress, apples, spinach and fennel.

4.   Pour the juice into tall glasses and if preferred dilute with a little water or ice.

5.   Serve immediately.

Spiced Crush

Just a dash of a spicy sauce can give a hint of sweet and sour to juices.

A source of vitamins C and E, beta-carotene, calcium and potassium.

Serves 2-3

6 tomatoes
½ pineapple
1 grapefruit
Worcestershire sauce
Chilled still or sparkling water
Crushed ice or ice cubes

1. Remove the stalks from the tomatoes and halve if large.

2. Slice the leaves and base off the pineapple and cut away the peel. Roughly chop the flesh.

3. Remove the outer peel from the grapefruit, leaving behind the white pith, and cut into wedges.

4. Juice the tomatoes, pineapple and grapefruit.

5. Flavour the juice with a few drops of Worcestershire sauce.

6. Pour the juice into tall glasses and if preferred dilute with a little water or ice.

7. Serve immediately.

Beetroot, Cranberry and Celery

The whole of a beetroot is edible. For variation add a few beetroot leaves.

A source of vitamin C, beta-carotene, calcium, folic acid, iron and potassium.

Serves 1-2

4 beetroots
2 oranges
1 handful cranberries
2 celery sticks
Chilled still or sparkling water
Crushed ice or ice cubes

1. Roughly slice the beetroots.

2. Remove the outer peel from the oranges, leaving behind the white pith, and cut into wedges.

3. Juice the beetroots, oranges, cranberries and celery.

4. Pour the juice into tall glasses and if preferred dilute with a little water or ice.

5. Serve immediately.

Cucumber and Melon Cooler

Very cooling and refreshing on a hot day. I enjoy this best as a long drink.

A source of vitamins A, B complex and C, folic acid and potassium.

Serves 3-4

1 cucumber
1 honeydew melon
4 spring onions
1 handful parsley
Chilled still or sparkling water
Crushed ice or ice cubes

1. Trim both ends of the cucumber and cut in half lengthways.

2. Cut the melon into wedges and scoop out and discard the seeds. Cut the flesh away from the skin and roughly chop.

3. Trim the ends of the spring onions.

4. Juice the parsley, cucumber, melon and spring onions.

5. Pour the juice into tall glasses and if preferred dilute with a little water or ice.

6. Serve immediately.

Carrot, Spinach and Chilli

If chillies are too hot replace with 3-5 radishes with their leaves. They will add a hot peppery flavour not quite as intense as chilli.

A source of vitamin A, folic acid, iron, magnesium and potassium.

Serves 1-2

2 carrots
3 green apples
1 green chilli
2 handfuls spinach leaves
Chilled still or sparkling water
Crushed ice or ice cubes

1. Scrub the carrots and remove both ends. Cut into chunks.

2. Remove the stalks from the apples and cut into wedges.

3. Cut the chilli in half and remove the stalk and seeds. (Take care not to touch your face when handling chillies.)

4. Juice the spinach, chilli, carrots and apples.

5. Pour the juice into tall glasses and if preferred dilute with a little water or ice.

6. Serve immediately.

Broccoli, Carrot and Apple

Choose crisp, fresh, green broccoli as this has the most nutrients.

A source of vitamins A and C, folic acid, iron and potassium.

Serves 1-2

4 green eating apples
5 carrots
3 beetroot leaves
3 broccoli florets
Chilled still or sparkling water
Crushed ice or ice cubes

1. Remove the stalks from the apples and cut into wedges.

2. Scrub the carrots and remove both ends. Cut into chunks.

3. Juice the beetroot leaves, apples, broccoli florets and carrots.

4. Pour the juice into tall glasses and if preferred dilute with a little water or ice.

5. Serve immediately.

Carrot, Kale and Celery

Select leaves of kale which are crisp, fresh and dark coloured.

A source of vitamins A, C and E, folic acid, magnesium and potassium.

Serves 1-2

8 carrots
A few parsley sprigs
3 kale leaves
3 celery sticks
Chilled still or sparkling water
Crushed ice or ice cubes

1. Scrub the carrots and remove both ends. Cut into chunks.

2. Juice the parsley, carrots, kale and celery.

3. Pour the juice into tall glasses and if preferred dilute with a little water or ice.

4. Serve immediately.

Radish, Beetroot and Carrot

A few radishes liven up savoury juices with their pleasing, peppery flavour.

A source of vitamins A and C, beta-carotene, calcium, carotenoids, folic acid, iron, magnesium and potassium.

Serves 2-3

4 carrots
1 beetroot
1 garlic clove
8 radishes with leaves
Chilled still or sparkling water
Crushed ice or ice cubes

1. Scrub the carrots and remove both ends. Cut into chunks.

2. Roughly chop the beetroot.

3. Juice the garlic, radishes, beetroot and carrots.

4. Pour the juice into tall glasses and if preferred dilute with a little water or ice.

5. Serve immediately.

Garlic Tomatoes

Mooli has a milder flavour than traditional red radishes and gives a more understated flavour to juices.

A source of vitamins A, C and E, beta-carotene, folic acid, phosphorus and potassium.

Serves 1-2

6 tomatoes
1 lettuce
5cm/2 inch mooli (white radish)
4 parsley sprigs
1 garlic clove
Crushed ice or ice cubes

1. Remove the stalks from the tomatoes and halve if large.

2. Cut away the lettuce root.

3. Roughly chop the mooli.

4. Juice the parsley sprigs, garlic, tomatoes, lettuce and mooli.

5. Pour the juice into tall glasses and if preferred chill with a little ice.

6. Serve immediately.

Peppered Tomatoes and Strawberries

A little black pepper enhances the flavour of both strawberries and tomatoes.

A source of vitamins C and E, beta-carotene, iron and potassium.

Serves 1-2

8 tomatoes
10 strawberries
1 yellow pepper
8 mint leaves
Chilled still or sparkling water
Crushed ice or ice cubes
Freshly ground black pepper

1. Remove the stalks from the tomatoes and halve if large.

2. Pull the green tops from the strawberries.

3. Halve the pepper, remove the stalk and the seeds. Cut the pepper into wedges.

4. Juice the mint, tomatoes, strawberries and yellow pepper.

5. Pour the juice into tall glasses and if preferred dilute with a little water or ice.

6, Sprinkle over a little ground pepper and serve immediately.

Apple Refresher

A refreshing drink for any time of the day using readily available ingredients.

A source of vitamin C, beta-carotene, flavonoids, folic acid, natural sugars, phosphorus and potassium.

Serves 1-2

6 green eating apples
Small bunch seedless green grapes
1 cucumber
1 kiwi fruit
½ lemon
Chilled still or sparkling water
Crushed ice or ice cubes

1. Remove the stalks from the apples and cut into wedges.

2. Take the grapes off the stalks.

3. Trim both ends of the cucumber and cut in half lengthways.

4. Peel the kiwi fruit and cut in half.

5. Remove the outer peel from the lemon, leaving behind the white pith, and cut into wedges.

6. Juice the lemon, kiwi fruit, apples, grapes and cucumber.

7. Pour the juice into tall glasses and if preferred dilute with a little water or ice.

8. Serve immediately.

Spinach, Orange and Alfalfa Sprouts

Alfalfa sprouts are available from good healthfood shops although they are very easy to grow in your home for a plentiful supply.

A source of vitamins A, B complex, C, E and K, beta-carotene, flavonoids, calcium, iron, folic acid.

Serves 1-2

3 oranges
½ lime
1 large handful spinach leaves
1 large handful alfalfa leaves
8 watercress sprigs
Chilled still or sparkling water
Crushed ice or ice cubes

1. Remove the outer peel from the oranges and lime, leaving behind the white pith, and cut into wedges.

2. Juice the spinach, alfalfa, watercress, oranges and lime.

3. Pour the juice into tall glasses and if preferred dilute with a little water or ice.

4. Serve immediately.

Liquid Salad

A deliciously healthy traditional salad combination, all contained in one glass.

A source of vitamins C and E, beta-carotene, flavonoids, calcium, folic acid, potassium and zinc.

Serves 2-3

6 tomatoes
2 oranges
½ red pepper
½ cucumber
3 spring onions
1 lettuce heart
2 celery sticks
Chilled still or sparkling water
Crushed ice or ice cubes

1. Remove the stalks from the tomatoes and halve if large.

2. Remove the outer peel from the oranges, leaving behind the white pith, and cut into wedges.

3. Remove the stalk from the pepper and scrape out the seeds. Cut the pepper into wedges.

4. Trim both ends of the cucumber and cut in half lengthways.

5. Trim the ends of the spring onions.

6. Juice the lettuce, celery, spring onions, tomatoes, oranges, pepper and cucumber.

7. Pour the juice into tall glasses and if preferred dilute with a little water or ice.

8. Serve immediately.

Sweet Potato and Orange

Flavours of the Deep South.

A source of vitamins C and E, beta-carotene, flavonoids, calcium, carotenoids, iron and protein.

Serves 1-2

350g/12 oz sweet potatoes
2 oranges
½ lemon
¼ cantaloupe melon
2 celery sticks
Chilled still or sparkling water
Crushed ice or ice cubes

1.   Peel the sweet potatoes and cut into chunks.

2.   Remove the outer peel from the oranges and lemon, leaving behind the white pith, and cut into wedges.

3.   Cut the melon into wedges and scoop out and discard the seeds. Cut the flesh away from the skin and roughly chop.

4.   Juice the sweet potatoes, oranges, lemon, melon and celery.

5.   Pour the juice into tall glasses and if preferred dilute with a little water or ice.

6.   Serve immediately.

Earthy Roots

Winter vegetables give a rich earthy flavour to this juice.

A source of vitamins A, B complex and E, folic acid, magnesium and potassium.

Serves 1-2

8 carrots
1 parsnip
¼ celeriac
2 small turnips
Tiny piece of horseradish root
Chilled still or sparkling water
Crushed ice or ice cubes
1 tsp toasted sesame seeds

1. Scrub the carrots and remove both ends. Cut into chunks.

2. Peel the parsnip, celeriac and turnips. Cut into chunks.

3. Juice the carrots, parsnip, celeriac, turnips and horseradish root.

4. Pour the juice into tall glasses and if preferred dilute with a little water or ice.

5. Sprinkle some toasted sesame seeds on top and serve immediately.

Nectarine, Tomato and Melon

Being rich in vitamins, melon is good for the skin.

A source of vitamins C and E, beta-carotene, flavonoids, folic acid and potassium.

Serves 1-2

4 tomatoes
3 nectarines
1 ogen melon
1 handful fresh coriander leaves
Pinch ground nutmeg
Chilled still or sparkling water
Crushed ice or ice cubes

1. Remove the stalks from the tomatoes and slice in half if large.

2. Cut the nectarines in half, remove the stones and slice the flesh.

3. Cut the melon into wedges and scoop out and discard the seeds. Cut the flesh away from the skin and roughly chop.

4. Finely chop the coriander leaves.

5. Juice the tomatoes, nectarines and melon.

6. Pour the juice into tall glasses and stir in the chopped coriander and a pinch of ground nutmeg.

7. If preferred dilute with a little water or ice and serve immediately.

Grapefruit and Lime Sherbet

A fizzy uplifting juice. For a 'pink' version use a ruby grape-fruit and black grapes.

A source of vitamin C, beta-carotene, flavonoids, folic acid, natural sugars and potassium.

Serves 1-2

1 grapefruit
½ lime
½ cucumber
Small bunch seedless green grapes
1 punnet cress
Sparkling water
Crushed ice or ice cubes

1. Remove the outer peel from the grapefruit and lime, leaving behind the white pith, and cut into wedges.

2. Trim both ends of the cucumber and roughly chop.

3. Take the grapes off the stalks.

4. Trim the roots of the cress.

5. Juice the cress, grapefruit, lime, cucumber and grapes.

6. Pour the juice into tall glasses and if preferred dilute with a little water or ice.

7. Serve immediately.

Spinach, Nettle and Pepper

You'll probably find young nettle leaves in your garden; make sure they haven't been sprayed with chemicals.

A source of vitamins A, C and E, beta-carotene, folic acid, iron, magnesium and potassium.

Serves 1-2

1 green pepper
3 carrots
4 tomatoes
Handful spinach leaves
10-15 nettle leaves
Chilled still or sparkling water
Crushed ice or ice cubes

1. Halve the pepper, remove the stalk and scrape out the seeds. Cut the pepper into wedges.

2. Scrub the carrots and remove both ends. Cut into chunks.

3. Remove the stalks from the tomatoes and halve if large.

4. Juice the spinach, pepper, nettles, tomatoes and carrots.

5. Pour the juice into tall glasses and if preferred dilute with a little water or ice.

6. Serve immediately.

Rocket, Pear and Apple

Rocket or arugula is a popular Italian salad leaf but also a traditional English salad plant, though only recently come back into fashion. With a peppery mustard flavour it is readily available in supermarkets.

A source of vitamin C, beta-carotene, folic acid, phosphorus and potassium.

Serves 1-2

2 green eating apples
3 pears
10 rocket leaves
2 celery sticks
Chilled still or sparkling water
Crushed ice or ice cubes

1. Remove the stalks from the apples and pears and cut into wedges.

2. Juice the rocket leaves, celery, apples and pears.

3. Pour the juice into tall glasses and if preferred dilute with a little water or ice.

4. Serve immediately.

Harvest Festival

A late summer extravaganza.

A source of vitamins A and C, beta-carotene, folic acid, magnesium, phosphorus and potassium.

Serves 2-3

4 carrots
2 green eating apples
1 courgette
6 parsley sprigs
5 cauliflower florets
Chilled still or sparkling water
Crushed ice or ice cubes

1. Scrub the carrots and remove both ends. Cut into chunks.

2. Remove the stalks from the apples and cut into wedges.

3. Trim both ends of the courgette and cut into chunks.

4. Juice the parsley, carrots, apples, courgette and cauliflower.

5. Pour the juice into tall glasses and if preferred dilute with a little water or ice.

6. Serve immediately.

Mango and Pineapple Cooler

Apple is a good base juice for both sweet and savoury juices.

A source of vitamin C, beta-carotene, folic acid, phosphorus and potassium.

Serves 2

1 mango
1 small pineapple
2 green eating apples
A few mint sprigs
Small piece fresh root ginger
Chilled still or sparkling water
Crushed ice or ice cubes

1. Thinly peel the mango and cut the flesh away from the stone.

2. Slice the leaves and base off the pineapple and cut away the peel. Cut two finger-sized pieces for decoration and roughly chop the remainder.

3. Remove the stalks from the apples and cut into wedges.

4. Juice the sprigs of mint, mango, pineapple, apples and ginger.

5. Pour the juice into tall glasses and if preferred dilute with a little water or ice.

6. Add a finger of pineapple to each glass and serve immediately.

Papaya, Strawberry and Raspberry

The seeds in a papaya are edible, but they have a peppery flavour so I have discarded them for this recipe.

A source of vitamins C and E, beta-carotene and flavonoids.

Serves 1-2

225g/8 oz strawberries
1 papaya
1 red eating apple
175g/6 oz raspberries
Chilled still or sparkling water
Crushed ice or ice cubes
1-2 tbsp thick Greek yoghurt

1. Remove the green tops from the strawberries.

2. Cut the papaya into wedges and scoop out the seeds. Slice the flesh from the peel.

3. Remove the stalk from the apple and cut into wedges.

4. Juice the strawberries, papaya, apple and raspberries.

5. Pour the juice into tall glasses and if preferred dilute with a little water or ice.

6. Top each glass with a spoonful of yoghurt and serve immediately.

Lychee and Nectarine Zinger

Lychees are a familiar Chinese fruit with a rough bright red shell. They will keep for a week if refrigerated.

A source of vitamin C, beta-carotene, flavonoids and potassium.

Serves 1

8 lychees
4 nectarines
¼ lime
Crushed ice or ice cubes
Gin

1. Remove the outer peel from the lychees and cut the flesh away from the stones.

2. Cut the nectarines in half, remove the stones and slice the flesh.

3. Remove the outer peel from the lime, leaving behind the white pith.

4. Juice the lychees, nectarines and lime.

5. Put some crushed ice into a tall glass and pour over the juice.

6. Stir in gin to flavour and serve immediately.

Redcurrant, Grape and Orange Juice

Fresh redcurrants are only available for a short time so I sometimes make this juice with frozen fruit.

A source of vitamin C, flavonoids, calcium, folic acid, iron and natural sugars.

Serves 1

175g/6 oz redcurrants
Small bunch seedless red grapes
2 oranges
Chilled still or sparkling water
Crushed ice or ice cubes
2 basil leaves

1. Take the redcurrants and grapes off the stalks.

2. Remove the outer peel from the oranges, leaving behind the white pith, and cut into wedges.

3. Juice the redcurrants, grapes and oranges.

4. Pour the juice into tall glasses and if preferred dilute with a little water or ice.

5. Float the basil leaves on the juice and serve immediately.

Prune and Orange Flip

It may seem unusual to juice dried fruit but it often has very intense flavours.

A source of vitamin C, beta-carotene, flavonoids, calcium, folic acid, iron, phosphorus and potassium.

Serves 1-2

85g/3 oz ready-to-eat dried prunes
1 Earl Grey tea bag
150ml/¼ pint mineral water
3 oranges
2 green eating apples
Crushed ice or ice cubes

1. Put the prunes and the tea bag into a small pan and pour over the mineral water.

2. Bring to the boil then remove from the heat and pour into a small bowl. Leave until cold.

3. Remove the tea bag and chill for one hour.

4. Remove the outer peel from the oranges, leaving behind the white pith, and cut into wedges.

5. Remove the stalks from the apples and cut into wedges.

6. Juice the wedges of orange and apple, alternating with the prunes and any soaking liquid. As the prunes will be soft, alternating them with the firmer fruit will help to force them through the juicer.

7. Pour the juice into a glass and if preferred add a little water and ice.

8. Serve immediately.

Blueberries, Peach and Apple

Look for round smooth-skinned blueberries, they will have the most juice. Discard any which are shrivelled.

A source of vitamins C and E, beta-carotene, folic acid, magnesium, phosphorus and potassium.

Serves 2

4 peaches
4 green eating apples
2 red eating apples
175g/6 oz blueberries
Chilled still or sparkling water
Crushed ice or ice cubes

1.	Cut the peaches in half, remove the stones and slice the flesh.

2.	Remove the stalks from the green and red apples and cut into wedges.

3.	Juice the peaches, green and red apples and blueberries.

4.	Pour the juice into glasses and if preferred add a little water and ice.

5.	Serve immediately.

Guava, Melon and Cucumber Blitz

Just one guava will add a sweet fragrant tropical flavour to a juice.

A source of vitamins A and C, folic acid and potassium.

Serves 1-2

1 guava
¼ honeydew melon
½ cucumber
Chilled still or sparkling water
Crushed ice or ice cubes

1. Cut the guava into wedges.

2. Scoop the seeds from the wedge of melon and discard. Cut the flesh away from the skin and roughly chop.

3. Trim both ends of the cucumber and cut in half lengthways.

4. Juice the guava, melon and cucumber.

5. Pour the juice into glasses and if preferred add a little water and ice.

6. Serve immediately.

Citrus Soother

Based on an old-fashioned remedy for sore throats this juice is always soothing and not exclusively medicinal.

A source of vitamin C, flavonoids, calcium, folic acid, and iron.

Serves 1

2 oranges
1 ruby grapefruit
1 lemon
3 sage leaves
Clear honey
Chilled still or sparkling water
Crushed ice or ice cubes

1. Remove the outer peel from the oranges, grapefruit and lemon, leaving behind the white pith, and cut into wedges.

2. Juice the sage leaves, oranges, grapefruit and lemon.

3. Pour the juice into a glass and sweeten with a little honey.

4. If preferred add a little water and ice and serve immediately.

Four Berries

A power juice full of nutrients.

A source of vitamins C and E, beta-carotene, folic acid, magnesium, phosphorus and potassium.

Serves 2

3 green eating apples
85g/3 oz blackberries
175g/6 oz raspberries
175g/6 oz blueberries
85g/3 oz cranberries
Chilled still or sparkling water
Crushed ice or ice cubes

1. Remove the stalks from the apples and cut into wedges.

2. Remove any stalks from the blackberries.

3. Juice the apples, blackberries, raspberries, blueberries and cranberries.

4. Pour the juice into glasses and if preferred add a little water and ice.

5. Serve immediately.

Fruit Fantasy

A juice with an amazing fruity flavour. Be wicked and add a scoop of vanilla ice cream to each serving to make a fruit float.

A source of vitamins C and E, beta-carotene, antioxidants, natural sugars, iron and potassium.

Serves 1-2

½ small pineapple
Small bunch seedless green grapes
3 apricots
2 red plums
1 persimmon
Chilled still or sparkling water
Crushed ice or ice cubes

1. Slice the leaves and base off the pineapple and cut away the peel. Roughly chop the flesh

2. Take the grapes off the stalks.

3. Cut the apricots and plums in half and remove the stones.

4. Remove the stalk from the persimmon and cut into wedges.

5. Juice the pineapple, grapes, apricots, plums and persimmon.

6. Pour the juice into glasses and if preferred add a little water and ice.

7. Serve immediately.

Orange and Mango Passion

Passion fruit gives a sweet tart flavour to juices with a hint of the tropics.

A source of vitamin C, flavonoids, calcium, folic acid, iron and potassium.

Serves 2-3

1 mango
6 oranges
½ lime
4 passion fruit
Chilled still or sparkling water
Crushed ice or ice cubes
8 fresh basil leaves

1. Thinly peel the mango and cut the flesh away from the stone.

2. Remove the outer peel from the oranges and lime, leaving behind the white pith, and cut into wedges.

3. Halve the passion fruit and scoop out the flesh and seeds.

4. Juice the mango, oranges, lime and passion fruit.

5. Pour the juice into glasses and if preferred add a little water and ice.

6. Float the basil leaves on top of the juice and serve immediately.

Peach, Plum and Mandarin

A scented juice, and when topped up with wine it's perfect for a 'drinks do' or as an apéritif.

A source of vitamins C and E, beta-carotene, flavonoids, calcium, folic acid and potassium.

Serves 3-4

5 peaches
5 plums
6 mandarin oranges
½ lime
Crushed ice or ice cubes
Dry white wine
3-4 borage or mint leaves

1. Cut the peaches in half, remove the stones and slice the flesh.

2. Cut the plums in half and remove the stones.

3. Remove the outer peel from the mandarin oranges and lime, leaving behind the white pith, and cut into wedges.

4. Juice the peaches, plums, mandarin oranges and lime.

5. Put crushed ice into tall glasses and pour over the juice.

6. Top up the glasses with dry white wine.

7. Decorate with borage or mint leaves and serve immediately.

Kiwi, Pineapple and Strawberry

Lemon balm leaves will add a subtle lemon flavour to the juice. If you don't have any to hand, substitute a few drops of lemon or lime juice.

A source of vitamins C and E, beta-carotene, folic acid, phosphorus and potassium.

Serves 2

1 small pineapple
350g/12 oz strawberries
4 kiwi fruit
2 green apples
10 lemon balm leaves
Chilled still or sparkling water
Crushed ice or ice cubes

1. Slice the leaves and base off the pineapple and cut away the peel. Roughly chop the flesh.

2. Remove the green tops from the strawberries.

3. Peel the kiwi fruit and cut into wedges.

4. Remove the stalks from the apples and cut into wedges.

5. Juice the lemon balm leaves, pineapple, strawberries, kiwi fruit and apples.

6. Pour the juice into tall glasses and if preferred add a little water and ice.

7. Serve immediately.

Cherry and Orange Shake

It may seem time-consuming having to stone cherries but cherry juice has a wonderful flavour which makes the effort worthwhile.

A source of vitamin C, flavonoids, calcium, folic acid, iron, magnesium and potassium.

Serves 4-6

175g/6 oz cherries
4 large oranges
Angostura bitters
Champagne, sparkling white wine or soda water
Crushed ice or ice cubes

1.   Pull the woody stalks from the cherries and remove the stones.

2.   Remove the outer peel from the oranges, leaving behind the white pith, and cut into wedges.

3.   Juice the cherries and oranges.

4.   Pour the juice into glasses and stir in a dash of Angostura bitters.

5.   Top up the glasses with Champagne, sparkling white wine or soda water. If preferred add a little ice and serve immediately.

Pear, Apple and Grape

Pear juice oxidises very quickly to release its flavour and nutrients, so drink as soon as it's made.

A source of vitamin C, antioxidants, beta-carotene, natural sugars, phosphorus, potassium.

Serves 1-2

225g/8 oz seedless green grapes
4 green eating apples
4 pears
Chilled still or sparkling water
Crushed ice or ice cubes

1.   Take the grapes off the stalks.

2.   Remove the stalks from the apples and pears and cut both fruits into wedges.

3.   Juice the grapes, apples and pears.

4.   Pour the juice into glasses and if preferred add a little water and ice.

5.   Serve immediately.

Melon Madness

Each time you make this juice use different melons. With their distinctive flavours it will be like a new recipe.

A source of vitamins A and C, flavonoids, calcium, folic acid, iron and potassium.

Serves 4

¼ **galia melon**
¼ **cantaloupe melon**
1 ogen melon
2 oranges
Small piece of root ginger
Chilled still or sparkling water
Crushed ice or ice cubes
Ground cinnamon

1.   Cut the galia, cantaloupe and ogen melons into wedges and scoop out and discard the seeds. Cut the flesh away from the skin and roughly chop.

2.   Remove the outer peel from the oranges, leaving behind the white pith, and cut into wedges.

3.   Juice the ginger, three melons and oranges.

4.   Pour the juice into tall glasses and if preferred add a little water and ice.

5.   Sprinkle a little cinnamon over each drink and serve immediately.

Apricot, Lime and Pomegranate

Juicing is the best way to extract the full flavour of pomegranates.

A source of vitamin C, beta-carotene, iron and potassium.

Serves 1-2

8 apricots
3 green eating apples
½ lime
1 pomegranate
Chilled still or sparkling water
Crushed ice or ice cubes

1. Cut the apricots in half and remove the stones.

2. Remove the stalks from the apples and cut into wedges.

3. Remove the outer peel from the lime, leaving the white pith behind, then cut into wedges.

4. Cut the pomegranate in half and scoop out the seeds. Reserve 2 tbsp of the seeds for decoration.

5. Juice the apricots, apples, lime and pomegranate seeds.

6. Pour the juice into tall glasses and if preferred add a little water and ice.

7. Stir in the reserved pomegranate seeds and serve immediately.

Orange, Apricot and Rose

I often use orange blossom water in place of the rosewater. Both add a fragrant perfume to juices and are available in good supermarkets.

A source of vitamin C, beta-carotene, flavonoids, calcium, folic acid, iron and potassium.

Serves 1

3 large oranges
6 apricots
Rosewater
Chilled still or sparkling water
Crushed ice or ice cubes

1. Remove the outer peel from the oranges, leaving behind the white pith, and cut into wedges.

2. Cut the apricots in half and remove the stones.

3. Juice the oranges and apricots.

4. Pour the juice into a glass and stir in a splash of rosewater to taste.

5. If preferred add a little water and ice and serve immediately.

Mango and Ginger Soda

A refreshing long fruity drink. You can replace the soda water with mineral or tonic water, or dry white wine.

A source of vitamin C, beta-carotene, flavonoids, and potassium.

Serves 1-2

1 mango
3 green eating apples
Small piece root ginger
1 celery stick
Soda water
Crushed ice or ice cubes
Celery leaves, to decorate

1. Thinly peel the mango and cut the flesh away from the stone.

2. Remove the stalks from the apples and cut into wedges.

3. Juice the ginger, mango, apples and celery.

4. Pour the juice into tall glasses. Top up the glasses with soda water and a little ice.

5. Add a few celery leaves to each glass and serve immediately.

Cranberry Kiss

Impress your guests with this home-made cocktail.

A source of vitamin C, beta-carotene and flavonoids.

Serves 4

2 pink grapefruits
175g/6 oz cranberries
5 tbsp Marsala
3 tbsp brandy
Crushed ice or ice cubes

1. Remove the outer peel from the grapefruits, leaving behind the white pith, and cut into wedges.

2. Juice the grapefruits and cranberries.

3. Pour the juice into a jug and stir in the Marsala and brandy.

4. Pour the juice mix into tall glasses and if preferred add a little ice.

5. Serve immediately.

Grape, Orange and Strawberry

Grapes add natural sweetness to juices.

A source of vitamins C and E, antioxidants, beta-carotene, folic acid, iron and natural sugars.

Serves 1-2

350g/12 oz Muscat grapes
225g/8 oz strawberries
1 orange
Chilled still or sparkling water
Crushed ice or ice cubes
Balsamic vinegar
Clear honey

1. Take the grapes off the stalks.

2. Remove the green tops from the strawberries.

3. Remove the outer peel from the orange, leaving behind the white pith, and cut into wedges.

4. Juice the grapes, strawberries and orange.

5. Pour the juice into tall glasses and if preferred add a little water and ice.

6. Stir a few drops of balsamic vinegar into each glass and sweeten with honey.

7. Serve immediately.

Banana, Peach and Nectarine

A thick power juice.

A source of vitamins A, B complex and C, beta-carotene, folic acid, magnesium, phosphorus and potassium.

Serves 1-2

1 peach
2 nectarines
2 green eating apples
1 ripe banana
Chilled still or sparkling water
Crushed ice or ice cubes

1. Cut the peach and nectarines in half, remove the stones and slice the flesh.

2. Remove the stalks from the apples and cut into wedges.

3. Juice the peach, nectarines and apples.

4. Mash the banana with a fork or potato masher, alternatively you could use a blender.

5. Slowly mix the juice into the mashed banana and pour into tall glasses. If preferred add a little water and ice.

6. Serve immediately.

Mango, Melon and Lavender

A few leaves of lavender will add an interesting hint of flavour to this juice. Rosemary could be used in the same way.

A source of vitamins A and C, beta-carotene, folic acid, phosphorus and potassium.

Serves 2-3

1 mango
4 green eating apples
¼ honeydew melon
10 lavender leaves
Chilled still or sparkling water
Crushed ice or ice cubes

1. Thinly peel the mango and cut the flesh away from the stone.

2. Remove the stalks from the apples and cut into wedges.

3. Scoop the seeds from the melon and discard. Cut the flesh away from the skin and roughly chop.

4. Juice the lavender leaves, mango, apples and melon.

5. Pour the juice into tall glasses and if preferred add a little water and ice.

6. Serve immediately.

Peach, Orange and Redcurrant

Along with apple, orange is a good base for juices, complementing other fruit flavours such as those in this recipe.

A source of vitamin C, beta-carotene, flavonoids, calcium, folic acid and iron.

Serves 1-2

2 peaches
3 large oranges
15-20 redcurrant berries
Chilled still or sparkling water
Crushed ice or ice cubes

1. Cut the peaches in half, remove the stones and slice the flesh.

2. Remove the outer peel from the oranges, leaving the white pith behind, and cut into wedges.

3. Juice the peaches, oranges and redcurrants.

4. Pour the juice into a glass and if preferred add a little water and ice.

5. Serve immediately.

Blackcurrant Fizz

There are many variations to this fizz. You could replace the blackcurrants with blackberries, redcurrants or loganberries.

A source of vitamin C, beta-carotene, folic acid, phosphorus and potassium.

Serves 1-2

2 green eating apples
2 red eating apples
¼ lime
225g/8 oz blackcurrants
Clear honey
Sparkling water, or white wine
Crushed ice or ice cubes

1. Take the stalks from the green and red apples and cut into wedges.

2. Remove the outer peel from the lime, leaving the white pith behind, and cut into wedges.

3. Pull the blackcurrants from the stalks.

4. Juice the apples, lime and blackcurrants.

5. Pour the juice into tall glasses and stir in a little of the honey to sweeten.

6. Top up the glasses with sparkling water or white wine and serve immediately.

7

RECIPES: JUICES, SMOOTHIES, ICES, SOUPS, ALCOHOLIC DRINKS AND MIXES

Beetroot and Orange Smoothie

Oranges and beetroots combined give drinks a wonderful colour.

A source of vitamins B complex and C, beta-carotene, calcium, folic acid, magnesium, potassium.

Serves 2-3

3 oranges
2 small beetroots
1 eating apple
Handful fresh coriander leaves
2 celery sticks
150ml/¼ pint Greek yoghurt
Chilled still or sparkling water
Crushed ice or ice cubes
Freshly ground black pepper

1. Remove the outer peel from the oranges, leaving behind the white pith, and cut into wedges.

2. Roughly slice the beetroots.

3. Remove the stalk from the apple and cut into wedges.

4. Juice the coriander leaves, oranges, beetroots, apple and celery.

5. Pour the juice into glasses and stir in the yoghurt.

6. Mix thoroughly and if preferred dilute with water or ice and serve immediately with a little pepper sprinkled on top.

Lime Salad Juice

For a slightly varied flavour each time you make this juice just use different mixes of salad leaves. You'll find some leaves are slightly more peppery or sweet than others.

A source of vitamins A and C, beta-carotene, calcium, folic acid, potassium, phosphorus.

Serves 3-4

1 lime
1 cucumber
2 eating apples
225g/8 oz packet of washed mixed salad leaves
6 sprigs fresh parsley
Crushed ice or ice cubes
3 tbsp vodka

1. Remove the outer peel from the lime, leaving behind the white pith, and cut into wedges.

2. Trim the ends off the cucumber and cut into chunks.

3. Remove the stalks from the apples and cut into wedges.

4. Juice the lime, cucumber, apples, salad leaves and parsley.

5. Put ice into glasses and pour over the vodka and juice.

6. Serve immediately.

Asparagus, Chicory and Orange

Green asparagus has a higher vitamin content than the white variety.

A source of vitamins A, B complex and C, flavonoids, folic acid, magnesium and potassium.

Serves 2

3 oranges
4 carrots
2 chicory heads
1 punnet mustard and cress
8 asparagus spears
1 tsp lemon juice

1. Remove the outer peel from the oranges, leaving the white pith, behind and cut into wedges.

2. Scrub the carrots and remove both ends. Cut into chunks.

3. Trim the chicory heads.

4. Cut the roots off the mustard and cress.

5. Juice the oranges, carrots, chicory, mustard and cress and asparagus spears.

6. Pour into two glasses, flavour with a little lemon juice and serve immediately.

Courgette, Cucumber and Lime

A refreshing drink for a hot day.

A source of vitamins C and E, beta-carotene, folic acid and potassium.

Serves 2

6 tomatoes
2 courgettes
1 cucumber
1 lime
Small piece of root ginger
150ml/¼ pint thick Greek yoghurt
4 tbsp milk
Crushed ice or ice cubes

1.   Remove the stalks from the tomatoes and halve if large.

2.   Trim both ends of the courgettes and the cucumber and cut them into chunks.

3.   Remove the outer peel from the lime, leaving the white pith behind, and cut into wedges.

4.   Juice the tomatoes, courgettes, cucumber, lime and ginger.

5.   Pour the juice into glasses and stir in the yoghurt and milk.

6.   Add a little ice for a cooler drink and serve immediately.

Veggie Four

Fennel gives a slight aniseed flavour.

A source of vitamin A, carotenoids, folic acid, iron, magnesium and potassium.

Serves 2

4 carrots
1 bulb fennel
3 broccoli florets
10 spinach leaves

1. Scrub the carrots and remove both ends. Cut into chunks.

2. Roughly chop the fennel.

3. Juice the carrots, fennel, broccoli and spinach.

4. Pour into small glasses and serve immediately.

Leafy Vegetable Juice

If you grow vegetables and herbs in pots, fresh leaves will always be available.

A source of vitamins A and C, beta-carotene, iron, folic acid, phosphorus and potassium.

Serves 1

1 handful spinach leaves   **4 sprigs fresh parsley**
1 handful lettuce leaves   **4 Swiss chard leaves**
6 dandelion leaves

1. Thoroughly wash all the leaves and chill for 20 minutes.

2. To juice the leaves roll a few together into tight balls and feed into the machine.

3. Pour the juice into a glass and serve immediately.

Pink Crush

Carrots and plums give this drink an almost sweet and sour flavour.

A source of vitamins A and C, carotenoids, calcium, folic acid, magnesium and potassium.

Serves 2

6 carrots
1 small beetroot
2 kiwi fruit
4 red plums
A few mint leaves

1. Scrub the carrots and remove both ends. Cut into chunks.

2. Roughly chop the beetroot.

3. Peel the kiwi fruit and cut in half.

4. Halve the plums and remove the stones.

5. Juice the mint leaves, carrots, beetroot, kiwi fruit and plums.

6. Pour into glasses and serve immediately.

Cucumber Lassi

A cooling Indian-style drink.

A source of vitamins A and C, calcium, folic acid, potassium, protein and zinc.

Serves 3-4

2 cucumbers
1 small shallot
10 mint leaves
A few coriander leaves
300ml/½ pint natural yoghurt
2 tbsp single cream
Ice cubes
1 tsp toasted cumin seeds
Ground black pepper
Celery leaves, to garnish

1. Trim both ends of the cucumbers and roughly chop.

2. Halve or quarter the shallot.

3. Juice the mint and coriander leaves with the cucumber and shallot.

4. Pour the juice into glasses and stir in the yoghurt and single cream.

5. Put one or two ice cubes in each glass and sprinkle over the cumin seeds and a little black pepper.

6. Garnish with celery leaves and serve immediately.

Breakfast Juice

A drink to wake you up in the morning.

A source of vitamins A and C, beta-carotene, antioxidants, folic acid, magnesium and potassium.

Serves 2-3

3 carrots
225g/8 oz seedless green grapes
3 pink grapefruits
2 celery sticks
Chilled still or sparkling water

1. Scrub the carrots and remove both ends. Cut into chunks.

2. Pull the grapes from the stalks.

3. Remove the outer peel from the grapefruits, leaving behind the white pith, then cut into wedges.

4. Juice the carrots, grapes, grapefruits and celery.

5. Pour into glasses and if preferred dilute with water and serve immediately.

Pepper Passion

The fiery flavour makes this drink an energy booster.

A source of vitamin C, calcium, beta-carotene, folic acid, iron, potassium and phosphorus.

Serves 2-3

½ red pepper
½ yellow pepper
2 green eating apples
1 handful spinach leaves
85g/3 oz tofu

1. Remove the stalks from the peppers and scrape out the seeds. Cut the peppers into wedges.

2. Remove the stalks from the apples and cut into wedges.

3. Juice the red and yellow peppers, apples and spinach leaves.

4. Put the tofu into a bowl and mix with a fork or whisk until smooth.

5. Slowly stir in the juice and pour into glasses.

6. Serve immediately.

Tomato and Basil Smoothie

Flavours of tomato and basil conjure images of sunny Italian holidays.

A source of vitamins C and E, beta-carotene, calcium, folic acid, potassium, phosphorus, protein and zinc.

Serves 2

14 cherry tomatoes
2 green eating apples
2 spring onions
10 basil leaves
Few drops Worcestershire sauce
300ml/½ pint natural yoghurt
4 ice cubes

1. Remove the stalks from the tomatoes and apples.

2. Cut the apples into wedges.

3. Trim the ends of the spring onions.

4. Juice the basil leaves, tomatoes, apples and spring onions.

5. Pour the juice into glasses and stir in the Worcestershire sauce and yoghurt.

6. Add the ice cubes and serve immediately.

Parsnip, Beetroot and Watercress

Parsnip gives a rich earthy flavour to this drink.

A source of vitamins B complex and C, beta-carotene, calcium, folic acid, and potassium.

Serves 2

1 large parsnip
3 small beetroots
3 green eating apples
½ cucumber
½ red pepper
1 handful watercress leaves
Crushed ice

1. Scrub the parsnip and remove both ends. Cut into chunks.

2. Roughly chop the beetroots.

3. Remove the stalks from the apples and cut into wedges.

4. Trim both ends of the cucumber and cut in half lengthways.

5. Remove the stalk from the pepper and scrape out the seeds. Cut the pepper into wedges.

6. Juice the parsnip, beetroots, apples, cucumber, pepper and watercress.

7. Pour into small glasses and add crushed ice.

8. Serve immediately.

Carrot Limeade

A long refreshing drink.

A source of vitamins A and C, flavonoids, calcium, folic acid, magnesium and potassium.

Serves 2-3

6 carrots
1 orange
1 lime
Small piece root ginger
1 tbsp chopped coriander leaves
Chilled sparkling water

1. Scrub the carrots and remove both ends. Cut into chunks.

2. Remove the outer peel from the orange and lime, leaving behind the white pith.

3. Juice the ginger, orange, lime and carrots.

4. Pour the juice into tall glasses and stir in the chopped coriander.

5. Top up the glasses with sparkling water.

6. Serve immediately.

Lettuce, Lemon and Tomato Refresher

A refreshing pick-me-up which I like to drink slightly chilled.

A source of vitamins A, C and E, beta-carotene, folic acid, phosphorus and potassium.

Serves 2-3

Small lemon wedge
1 Romaine lettuce
8 cherry tomatoes
Handful watercress leaves
Chilled still or sparkling water
Crushed ice or ice cubes

1. Remove the outer peel from the lemon, leaving behind the white pith.

2. Cut away the lettuce root.

3. Remove the stalks from the tomatoes.

4. Juice the lemon, lettuce, tomatoes and watercress.

5. If preferred dilute with water or ice and serve immediately.

Avocado, Apple and Carrot Thickie

A rich smooth extra-thick drink to revive the spirits.

A source of vitamins A, B complex, C and E, calcium, beta-carotene, folic acid, magnesium, potassium, proteins and zinc.

Serves 1

2 carrots
2 Golden Delicious apples
2 tomatoes
½ lemon
1 celery stick
1 small ripe avocado
2 tbsp natural yoghurt
Crushed ice

1. Scrub the carrots and remove both ends. Cut into chunks.

2. Remove the stalks from the apples and cut into wedges.

3. Remove the stalks from the tomatoes and slice in half if large.

4. Remove the outer peel from the lemon, leaving behind the white pith, and cut into wedges.

5. Juice the carrots, apples, tomatoes, lemon and celery stick.

6. Cut the avocado in half, remove the stone and scoop the flesh into a small bowl.

7. Mix the avocado flesh and the yoghurt together with a fork or whisk until smooth.

8. Slowly mix in the juice, add a little ice and serve immediately.

Hot Juice

Pepper, radishes and watercress give this drink lots of heat and peppery flavours. An energy booster to drink in small quantities.

A source of vitamin A, beta-carotene, calcium, folic acid and potassium.

Serves 2-3

1 red pepper
1 bunch radishes
4 green eating apples
2 beetroots
1 bunch watercress
Small handful fresh chives

1. Cut the pepper in half and remove the stalk and seeds. Cut the pepper into wedges.

2. Scrub the radishes and trim.

3. Remove the stalks from the apples and cut into wedges.

4. Cut the beetroots into rough chunks.

5. Juice the watercress and chives first then add the pepper, radishes, apples and beetroots.

6. Pour into small glasses and serve immediately.

Vegetable Cocktail

A feast of vegetables all in one glass.

A source of vitamins A, C and E, beta-carotene, folic acid, magnesium and potassium.

Serves 1

4 carrots
8 cherry tomatoes
1 beetroot
2 cabbage leaves
2 broccoli florets
1 celery stick

1. Scrub the carrots and remove both ends then cut into chunks.

2. Remove the stalks from the tomatoes.

3. Roughly chop the beetroot.

4. Juice the carrots, tomatoes, beetroot, cabbage, broccoli and celery.

5. Pour into a glass and serve immediately.

Herb and Tomato Crush

Choose tomatoes which are still on the vine, they will give a much better flavoured juice.

A source of vitamins A, C and E, beta-carotene, folic acid and potassium.

Serves 2-3

8 Italian plum tomatoes
3 carrots
½ red pepper
2 spring onions
Small handful mixed fresh herbs
½ garlic clove
Dry white wine (optional)

1. Remove the green tops from the tomatoes and cut them in half if they are large.

2. Scrub the carrots and trim both ends then cut into chunks.

3. Remove the seeds from the pepper and cut the pepper into wedges.

4. Trim the spring onions.

5. Juice the herbs, spring onions and garlic clove first and then add the tomatoes, carrots and pepper.

6. Pour the juice into glasses and for an extra kick mix in a little white wine.

7. Serve immediately.

Tofu Energizer

Wheatgrass is becoming very popular in health juices. I like to mix it with tofu or yoghurt.

A source of chlorophyll, beta-carotene, calcium, folic acid and iron.

Serves 2-3

2 handfuls wheatgrass
10 spinach leaves
4 sprigs fresh parsley
4 tbsp tofu
150ml/¼ pint non-dairy 'milk'

1. Juice the wheatgrass, spinach leaves and parsley.

2. Put the tofu into a jug and with a fork or whisk slowly stir in the non-dairy 'milk' until the mixture is smooth.

3. Mix in the juice and pour into small glasses.

4. Serve immediately.

Melon Bonanza

Melon juice is very refreshing and is delicious drunk through-out the day.

A source of vitamins A and C, antioxidants, folic acid, natural sugars, magnesium and potassium.

Serves 2-3

Small bunch green grapes
¼ small green melon
1 wedge watermelon
2 carrots
2 pears
2 celery sticks

1. Pull the grapes from the stalks.

2. Scoop the seeds from both the melons and discard. Cut the flesh from the peel.

3. Scrub the carrots and remove both ends then cut into chunks.

4. Remove the stalks from the pears and cut into wedges.

5. Juice the grapes, melons, carrots, pears and celery.

6. Pour into glasses and serve immediately.

Tomato and Pak Choi Cooler

Delicious cold but for a change heat and serve warm.

A source of vitamins A, C and E, flavonoids, beta-carotene, calcium, folic acid, iron and potassium.

Serves 2-3

2 oranges
8 firm tomatoes
2 spring onions
2 thin slices red pepper
2 pak choi
1 stick celery
2 tsp toasted sesame seeds
Crushed ice or ice cubes

1. Remove the outer peel from the oranges, leaving the white pith behind, then cut into wedges.

2. Remove the stalks from the tomatoes and halve or quarter if large.

3. Trim the ends off the spring onions and remove any seeds from the pepper.

4. Trim the pak choi and separate the leaves.

5. Juice the oranges, tomatoes, spring onions, pepper, pak choi and celery.

6. Scatter over the sesame seeds and chill in the fridge or add a little ice and serve immediately.

Green Passion

Even though many bags of leaves are pre-washed I would still give them a thorough rinse.

A source of vitamins C and E, beta-carotene, folic acid, potassium and phosphorus.

Serves 2-3

¼ cucumber
3 green eating apples
1 lemon wedge
Few parsley sprigs
Handful spinach leaves
Handful watercress leaves
Still or sparkling water

1. Trim both ends of the cucumber and cut into chunks.

2. Remove the stalks from the apples and cut them into wedges.

3. Remove the outer peel from the lemon wedge, leaving the white pith behind.

4. Juice the cucumber, apples, lemon, parsley, spinach and watercress leaves.

5. Pour the juice into glasses. This juice is thick and has a strong flavour so if preferred dilute with a little water.

6. Serve immediately.

Carrot and Orange Soup

Carrots don't need to be peeled but it is important to scrub them thoroughly and trim both ends.

A source of vitamins A, C and E, beta-carotene, flavonoids, folic acid, magnesium and potassium.

Serves 4-6

350g/12 oz carrots
2 oranges
1 orange pepper
4 tomatoes
½ red chilli
6 sprigs parsley
Salt and ground black pepper
150ml/¼ pint single cream (optional)
Chopped fresh parsley, to garnish

1. Scrub the carrots and remove both ends. Cut into chunks.

2. Remove the outer peel from the oranges, leaving behind the white pith, and cut into wedges.

3. Cut the pepper vertically into quarters, removing the stalk and seeds. Cut the pepper into wedges.

4. Remove the stalks from the tomatoes and slice in half if large.

5. Juice the chilli and parsley first and then add the carrots, oranges, pepper and tomatoes.

6. Pour the juice into a saucepan and stir in 300ml/½ pint water. Bring to the boil and season to taste.

7. Pour into soup bowls and swirl in a little cream. Sprinkle over some chopped parsley and serve immediately.

DIY Bloody Mary

A drink to perk you up at the end of a long, hard day.

A source of vitamins C and E, beta-carotene and potassium.

Serves 3-4

12 tomatoes
3 celery sticks with leaves
½ red chilli
1 clove garlic
4 tbsp vodka
Few drops lemon juice
Worcestershire sauce
Salt and ground black pepper
Crushed ice (optional)

1. Remove the tomato stalks and cut the tomatoes in half if large.

2. Reserve a few celery leaves for garnish.

3. Slice the chilli in half and carefully remove the seeds avoiding touching your face. The more chilli you use, the 'hotter' the drink.

4. Juice the chilli first with the garlic and tomatoes and then add the celery sticks.

5. Pour the juice into a jug and stir in the vodka and lemon juice.

6. Season to taste with Worcestershire sauce, salt and ground black pepper.

7. Pour into glasses, add a little ice and celery leaves and serve immediately.

Blueberry Breakfast

A healthy drink to start the day. In place of the blueberries you could use raspberries or mango.

A source of vitamin C, calcium, carotenoids, folic acid, phosphorus, protein, potassium and zinc.

Serves 2

3 crisp eating apples
2 kiwi fruit
225g/8 oz blueberries
2 tbsp thick Greek yoghurt
Whole or skimmed milk
Clear honey (optional)
2 tsp wheatgerm

1. Remove the apple stalks and cut the apples into wedges.

2. Quarter the kiwi fruit.

3. Juice the apples, kiwis and blueberries. Pour into two glasses.

4. Stir in the yoghurt and top up with milk.

5. If preferred sweeten with honey and sprinkle the wheatgerm on top.

6. Serve immediately.

Apricot and Clementine Drink

A delicious drink for those who prefer to avoid dairy products, although it could be made with cow's or goat's milk.

A source of vitamin C, beta-carotene, calcium, folic acid, flavonoids, iron and potassium.

Serves 2-3

8 apricots
3 clementines or satsumas
1 lime
Non-dairy 'milk'
Chilled still or sparkling water
Crushed ice or ice cubes
1 tbsp toasted sesame seeds

1. Cut the apricots in half and remove the stones.

2. Remove the outer peel from the clementines or satsumas and lime, leaving the white pith behind, then cut into wedges.

3. Juice the apricots, clementines or satsumas and lime and pour into glasses.

4. Top up the glasses with non-dairy 'milk' or if preferred a mix of 'milk' and still or sparkling water.

5. For a cold drink add a little ice then sprinkle over the toasted sesame seeds and serve immediately.

Nectarine, Peach and Plum Shake

Select firm fruit because it will give more juice.

A source of vitamins C and E, beta-carotene, calcium, flavonoids, folic acid, phosphorus, potassium, protein and zinc.

Serves 4

3 nectarines
3 peaches
6 red plums
2 red eating apples
Small piece fresh root ginger
4 tbsp thick Greek yoghurt
150ml/¼ pint milk
Mint leaves, to decorate

1. Cut the nectarines, peaches and plums in half and remove the stones.

2. Remove the stalks from the apples.

3. Cut all the fruit into wedges.

4. Juice the ginger first and then add the nectarines, peaches, plums and apples.

5. Pour the juices into a jug and mix in the yoghurt and milk.

6. Pour into glasses, decorate with mint leaves and serve immediately.

Cherry and Raspberry Yoghurt Drink

Yoghurt adds a tartness to drinks. If preferred sweeten with a little honey.

A source of vitamin C, calcium, flavonoids, magnesium, potassium, protein and zinc.

Serves 2-3

225g/8 oz cherries, plus 2 or 3 to decorate
225g/8 oz raspberries
150ml/¼ pint low fat natural yoghurt
4 tbsp skimmed milk
Mint leaves, to garnish

1. Pull the woody stalks from the cherries and remove the stones.

2. Juice the cherries and raspberries.

3. Pour the juice into a jug and stir in the yoghurt and milk.

4. Add a little more milk if a thinner drink is preferred.

5. Chill or pour into glasses and decorate each with a cherry and mint leaves.

6. Serve immediately.

Pineapple, Banana and Rum Float

A wonderful creamy alcoholic adult drink. Don't drink too many.

A source of vitamins A, B complex and C, beta-carotene, folic acid, magnesium, phosphorus and potassium.

Serves 2-3

3 eating apples
1 small pineapple or 4 slices of a regular-sized
  pineapple
2 bananas
1 tbsp rum or brandy
2 tbsp coconut cream
2 tbsp double cream
A few walnut pieces

1. Remove the stalks from the apples and cut into wedges.

2. Slice the leaves and base off the pineapple and cut away the peel. Roughly chop the flesh.

3. Mash the bananas with a fork or potato masher, or alternatively you could use a blender.

4. Juice the apples and pineapple.

5. Slowly stir the juices into the mashed banana.

6. Mix in the rum or brandy and pour into glasses.

7. Float the coconut cream carefully on top of the banana mixture. This is quite easy if the cream is slowly poured over an upturned spoon held just above the surface of the drink.

8. Scatter over the walnut pieces and serve immediately.

Tropical Smoothie

Everyone will love this juice with its exotic flavours reminiscent of happy holidays.

A source of vitamin C, beta-carotene and potassium.

Serves 3-4

1 pineapple
1 mango
½ lime
2-3 slices red chilli
4 tablespoons dry vermouth or vodka
4 tbsp coconut cream
Crushed ice

1. Slice the leaves and base off the pineapple and cut away the peel. Cut three or four finger-sized pieces for decoration and roughly chop the remainder.

2. Thinly peel the mango and cut the flesh away from the stone.

3. Thinly peel the lime and cut a few strips of peel for decoration.

4. Juice the chilli, lime and mango first and then add the roughly chopped pineapple.

5. Stir the vermouth or vodka and coconut cream into the juice.

6. Pour into glasses, add some crushed ice and the pineapple fingers then serve immediately.

Papaya, Strawberry and Marshmallow Froth

A fun drink. You'll probably need a spoon to scoop up the last pieces of marshmallow and chocolate.

A source of vitamins C and E, beta-carotene, calcium, flavonoids, phosphorus, potassium, protein and zinc.

Serves 4

1 ripe medium papaya
350g/12 oz strawberries
2 eating apples
Milk
Handful mini marshmallows
2 tsp grated chocolate

1. Cut the papaya into wedges and scoop out the seeds. Slice the flesh from the peel.

2. Remove the green tops from the strawberries.

3. Remove the stalks from the apples and cut into wedges.

4. Juice the papaya, strawberries and apples.

5. Pour the juice into glasses and stir in the milk.

6. Float some of the marshmallows on top and sprinkle over a little grated chocolate.

7. Serve immediately.

Grape, Melon and Cucumber Smoothie

A soothing drink, delicately perfumed with the flavours of melon and grapes.

A source of vitamins A and C, antioxidants, folic acid, natural sugars and potassium.

Serves 2-3

1 honeydew melon
350g/12 oz seedless red grapes
1 cucumber
10-12 mint leaves
Soya milk

1. Slice the melon into wedges and scoop out and discard the seeds. Cut the flesh away from the skin and roughly chop.

2. Take the grapes off the stalks.

3. Trim the ends off the cucumber and cut into chunks.

4. Juice the mint leaves first and then add the grapes, melon and cucumber.

5. Pour the juice into glasses and stir in the soya milk.

6. Serve immediately.

Passion Fruit and Mango Delight

It's easy to overlook passion fruit, they are brownish purple and wrinkled but inside the edible seeds are surrounded by orange flesh and have a wonderful tart, tropical flavour.

A source of vitamin C, beta-carotene, flavonoids, calcium, folic acid, iron, potassium, protein and zinc.

Serves 2-3

4 passion fruit
2 oranges
1 mango
Skimmed milk
Still or sparkling water
Crushed ice or ice cubes

1.   Halve the passion fruit and scoop the flesh and seeds from three of the fruit into the juicer.

2.   Remove just the outer peel from the oranges, leaving behind the white pith, then cut each into four.

3.   Thinly peel the mango and cut the flesh away from the stone.

4.   Juice the passion fruit and then add the oranges and mango.

5.   Pour the juice into glasses and top up with skimmed milk or still or sparkling water.

6.   Cut the remaining passion fruit in half and scoop some of the flesh and seeds on top of each glass.

Peach and Raspberry Ice Cream Float

A lively, colourful drink. Serve with straws and spoons so every drop is drunk.

A source of vitamin C, beta-carotene, flavonoids, potassium and folic acid.

Serves 3-4

3 peaches
350g/12 oz raspberries
5 oranges
4 scoops vanilla ice cream
Ice cubes
Fresh mint leaves, to decorate

1.   Cut the peaches in half, remove the stones and slice the flesh.

2.   Juice the peaches and the raspberries together and pour into tall glasses.

3.   Remove just the outer peel from the oranges, leaving behind the white pith, then cut each into wedges and juice.

4.   Carefully pour the orange juice into the glasses on top of the peach and raspberry juice. The juices will swirl together to give a marbled effect.

5.   Add a scoop of ice cream and a couple of ice cubes to each glass and garnish with mint leaves.

6.   Push a straw into each glass and serve immediately.

Liquid Sunshine Smoothie

This thick bright smoothie looks more of a meal than a drink.

A source of vitamin C, beta-carotene, folic acid, phosphorus and potassium.

Serves 2

1 mango
2 red eating apples
½ lime
350g/12 oz raspberries
100ml/3½ fl oz coconut cream
4 tbsp thick natural yoghurt
Still or sparkling water
Ice
Ground cinnamon, to sprinkle

1. Peel the mango and cut the flesh away from the stone.

2. Remove the stalks from the apples and cut into wedges.

3. Remove the outer peel from the lime, leaving the white pith behind.

4. Juice the mango, apples, lime and raspberries and pour into a jug.

5. Stir in the coconut cream and yoghurt and pour into tall glasses. If you prefer a thinner drink stir in a little water.

6. Add some ice, sprinkle over a little ground cinnamon and serve immediately.

Tomato, Mint and Melon Ice

Serve this savoury vodka ice as an unusual starter to a meal . . . a real talking point.

A source of vitamins A, C and E, beta-carotene, folic acid, and potassium.

Serves 4-6

450g/1 lb tomatoes
1 cantaloupe melon
Handful fresh mint leaves
1 clove garlic
150ml/¼ pint vodka or dry vermouth (optional)
4 celery sticks
Savoury biscuits, to serve

1. Remove the stalks from the tomatoes and cut in half.

2. Cut the melon into wedges and scoop out and discard the seeds. Cut the flesh away from the skin and roughly chop.

3. Juice the mint leaves and tomatoes first and then add the pieces of melon and garlic.

4. Pour the juice into a freezer container and stir in the vodka or vermouth or if you prefer water.

5. Very finely chop the celery and stir into the tomato mixture.

6. Freeze for an hour or until the mixture begins to ice around the edges.

7. Scrape the iced mixture from the edges and thoroughly mix. Return to the freezer for 20 minutes then mix again. Repeat this process once more then freeze until firm.

8. Spoon the ice into small glass dishes and serve immediately with savoury biscuits.

Pear and Banana Smoothie

You can't really juice a banana but if they are very ripe they'll mash down very easily with a fork.

A source of vitamins A and C, calcium, beta-carotene, folic acid, magnesium, potassium, protein and zinc.

Serves 2-3

2 apples
3 pears
2 ripe bananas
4 dried apricots
6 pecan nuts
150ml/¼ pint skimmed milk
Maple syrup, to taste
Crushed ice or ice cubes

1. Remove stalks from the apples and pears and cut both fruits into wedges.

2. Mash the bananas with a fork or potato masher, alternatively you could use a blender.

3. Finely chop the apricots and pecan nuts.

4. Juice the apples and pears and thoroughly mix with the mashed banana.

5. Stir in the milk and sweeten with maple syrup.

6. Pour into tall glasses and for a colder drink stir in a little ice.

7. Sprinkle the chopped apricots and nuts on top of each drink and serve immediately.

Cranberry, Apple and Watermelon

Cranberries are very tart so just a small amount will add a delicious refreshing flavour to the juice.

A source of vitamins A and C, beta-carotene, folic acid, phosphorus and potassium.

Serves 4-6

½ small watermelon
5 eating apples
½ lemon
2.5cm/1 inch piece of root ginger
85g/3 oz cranberries
4-6 small celery sticks, to decorate

1. Cut the watermelon into wedges and scoop out and discard the seeds. Cut the flesh from the skin and roughly chop.

2. Remove the stalks from the apples and cut into wedges.

3. Remove a very thin layer of outer peel from the lemon.

4. Juice the ginger, lemon and cranberries first and then add the apples and watermelon.

5. Pour the juice into tall glasses, add a celery stick and serve immediately.

Red Fruit Punch

A non-alcoholic party drink packed with juicy flavours.

A source of vitamins A, C and E, antioxidants, beta-carotene, magnesium and natural sugars.

Serves 10-12

350g/12 oz strawberries
350g/12 oz seedless black grapes
350g/12 oz blackberries
225g/8 oz raspberries
1 bottle non-alcoholic sparkling rosé wine
4 tbsp elderflower syrup
10 ice cubes
½ cucumber
1 blood orange
Mint leaves, to decorate

1. Remove the green tops from the strawberries and take the grapes off the stalks.

2. Juice the strawberries, grapes, blackberries and raspberries then pour the juice into a large bowl.

3. Pour in the sparkling rosé wine then stir in the elderflower syrup and ice cubes.

4. Thinly slice the cucumber and orange then float on top of the punch with the mint leaves.

5. Serve immediately.

Orange Creams

A very smooth comforting drink with a crisp crunchy topping.

A source of vitamin C, antioxidants, flavonoids, calcium, folic acid and natural sugars.

Serves 2-3

6 blood oranges
1 lemon
225g/8 oz seedless green grapes
2 tsp clear honey
150ml/¼ pint single cream
2-3 ice cubes
2 tbsp crushed peanut brittle

1. Remove the outer peel from the oranges and lemon, leaving the white pith behind, then cut into wedges.

2. Take the grapes off the stalks.

3. Juice the oranges, lemon and grapes and pour into wide shallow glasses.

4. Swirl some of the honey and cream into each glass and if you like add an ice cube.

5. Top with a little crushed peanut brittle and serve immediately.

Iced Fruit Smoothies

A useful recipe containing ingredients which are available all year round.

A source of vitamins C and E, beta-carotene, folic acid, magnesium, phosphorus and potassium.

Serves 4-6

4 eating apples
1 cucumber
450g/1 lb bag frozen mixed berries
2 ripe bananas
150ml/¼ pint skimmed milk

1. Remove the stalks from the apples and cut into wedges.

2. Trim the ends off the cucumber and cut into chunks.

3. Juice the apples, cucumber and the frozen berries and pour into a bowl.

4. Mash the bananas with a fork or potato masher, alternatively you could use a blender.

5. Slowly stir the juice into the mashed banana and mix in the milk.

6. Pour into glasses and serve immediately.

Plum and Cranberry Granita

Granita is an Italian ice, a frozen mix of fruit juices and flavourings, which freezes to an icy mass and is scraped with a spoon into glasses.

A source of vitamins C and E, beta-carotene, flavonoids, calcium, folic acid, iron and potassium.

Serves 4

450g/1 lb plums
4 oranges
1 lemon
4 apples
350g/12 oz cranberries
3 tbsp dessert wine or brandy
Clear honey, to taste
Sweet biscuits, to serve

1. Halve the plums and remove the stones.

2. Remove the outer peel from the oranges and lemon, leaving the white pith behind, then cut each into four.

3. Remove the stalks from the apples and cut them into wedges.

4. Juice the plums, oranges, lemon, apples and cranberries and pour into a freezer container.

5. Stir in the dessert wine or brandy and sweeten with honey.

6. Freeze for an hour or until the mixture begins to ice around the edges.

7. Scrape the iced mixture from the edges and thoroughly mix. Return to the freezer for 20 minutes then mix again. Repeat this process once more then freeze until firm.

8. Spoon the ice into small glass dishes and serve immediately with sweet biscuits.

Iced Earl Grey and Apricot Tea

Keep a jug of iced tea in the fridge; it is very refreshing especially on a hot day.

A source of vitamin C, flavonoids, beta-carotene, folic acid, iron and potassium.

Serves 4-6

3 Earl Grey tea bags
8 apricots
1 orange
1 lime
Clear honey or sugar, to taste
20 ice cubes
Mint leaves, to garnish

1. Put the tea bags into a large jug and pour over ½ pint of boiling water. Leave to infuse for 15 minutes then remove the tea bags. Chill the tea.

2. Halve the apricots and discard the stones.

3. Remove the outer peel from the orange, leaving behind the white pith, and cut into wedges.

4. Cut the lime in half. Remove the outer peel from one half. Slice the other half into four or six and reserve for decoration.

5. Juice the apricots, orange and the peeled lime.

6. Stir the juices into the tea and sweeten with honey or sugar to taste.

7. Mix in the ice cubes and chill until needed. Serve in glasses with a slice of lime and mint leaves.

Daisy Fizz Cocktail

An American-style cocktail with the freshness of home-juiced fruit.

A source of vitamin C, flavonoids, folic acid and potassium.

Serves 3-4

4 oranges
½ lemon
½ lime

2-3 measures brandy
6 crushed ice cubes
Soda water

1. Remove the outer peel from the oranges, lemon and lime.

2. Juice the oranges, lemon and lime and pour into tall glasses.

3. Stir the brandy and crushed ice into each glass.

4. Top up each glass with soda water and serve immediately.

Peach and Raspberry Bubbles

This is a delicate drink for very special occasions. A sparkling white wine can be used as an alternative to champagne.

A source of vitamin C, beta-carotene and potassium.

Serves 6-8

4 peaches
225g/8 oz raspberries

Pink champagne, chilled

1. Cut the peaches in half, remove the stones and slice the flesh.

2. Juice the peaches and raspberries and pour into champagne flutes.

3. Fill the glasses with pink champagne and serve immediately.

Sangria-Style Drink

There'll be non-stop partying with this Spanish-style drink.

A source of vitamin C, beta-carotene, flavonoids, calcium, folic acid, phosphorus and potassium.

Serves 8-10

5 oranges
1 grapefruit
10 red eating apples
4 pears
1 bottle dry red wine
2 tbsp brandy
Clear honey or icing sugar
3 limes
Crushed ice or ice cubes
Mint leaves, to decorate

1.   Remove the outer peel from the oranges and grapefruit, leaving behind the white pith, and cut the fruit into wedges.

2.   Remove the stalks from the apples and pears and cut the fruit into wedges.

3.   Juice the oranges, grapefruit, apples and pears.

4.   Pour the juices into a very large jug or bowl and stir in the red wine and brandy.

5.   If a sweeter drink is preferred stir in a little clear honey or icing sugar, to taste. (Allow time for the icing sugar to dissolve.)

6.   Thinly slice the limes then serve the drinks with plenty of ice and decorate the glasses with a slice of lime and mint leaves.

Rainbow Lollies

Children will love helping to make these pure-juice iced-lollies. They are the ideal natural sweet.

A source of vitamins C and E, beta-carotene, magnesium, phosphorus and potassium.

Makes 10-12

4 oranges
350g/12 oz strawberries
350g/12 oz blackberries
5 kiwi fruit
Sparkling water
Clear honey

1. You will need an iced-lolly mould or use clean small plastic yoghurt pots and small wooden skewers for the lolly sticks.

2. Remove just the outer peel from the oranges, leaving behind the white pith, then cut each into four.

3. Remove the green tops from the strawberries.

4. Juice each type of fruit separately and pour into four bowls.

5. If necessary add sparkling water to make each of the juices up to at least 300ml/½ pint and sweeten to taste with honey. Chill until needed.

6. Pour some orange juice into the moulds to give a shallow layer and freeze until set. Repeat with a different coloured juice gradually building layers of colour. Freeze until solid.

Chilled Orange and Strawberry Soup

Fruit soups are a popular Scandinavian delicacy.

A source of vitamins C and E, flavonoids, calcium, folic acid, iron and potassium.

Serves 4-6

6 blood oranges
450g/1 lb strawberries
1 cucumber
2.5cm/1 inch piece of root ginger
Clear honey, to taste
8 ice cubes
150ml/¼ pint Greek yoghurt

1. Remove the outer peel from the blood oranges, leaving the white pith behind, then cut into wedges.

2. Remove the green tops from the strawberries. Slice four to six and reserve for decoration.

3. Halve the cucumber lengthways.

4. Juice the blood oranges, strawberries, cucumber and ginger and pour into a bowl.

5. Sweeten to taste with honey and stir in the ice cubes. Chill for one or two hours.

6. Pour the chilled soup into bowls, add a swirl of yoghurt and float the reserved strawberry slices on top. Serve immediately.

Hot Plum and Melon Soup

Based on a Danish chilled soup, serve as a starter or a dessert.

A source of vitamins A, C and E, beta-carotene, folic acid, phosphorus and potassium.

Serves 4-6

12 plums
4 apples
1 medium-sized cantaloupe melon
4 tangerines
½ tsp ground cinnamon
Clear honey, to taste
150ml/¼ pint Greek yoghurt

1. Halve the plums and remove the stones.

2. Remove the stalks from the apples and cut into wedges.

3. Cut the melon into wedges and scoop out and discard the seeds. Cut the flesh away from the skin and roughly chop.

4. Remove the outer peel from the tangerines, leaving the white pith behind, then cut into wedges.

5. Juice the plums, apples, melon and tangerines and pour into a saucepan.

6. Stir in 300ml/½ pint water and the cinnamon. Bring almost to the boil and sweeten with honey, to taste.

7. Pour into soup bowls add a spoonful of yoghurt and serve immediately.

Fruit Cup

If you prefer, use your own favourite mix of fruit such as kiwi fruit, cherries, raspberries and mangoes.

A source of vitamins A, C and E, antioxidants, flavonoids, folic acid and potassium.

Serves 10-12

6 eating apples
4 pears
6 oranges
1 lime
350g (12 oz) seedless green grapes
2 bottles dry white wine
One wine glass Cointreau
Ice cubes (optional)
Mint or lemon balm leaves, to decorate

1. Remove the stalks from the apples and pears and cut both fruits into wedges.

2. Remove the outer peel from the oranges and lime, leaving the white pith behind, then cut into wedges.

3. Take the grapes off the stalks.

4. Juice the apples, pears, oranges, lime and grapes and pour into a large bowl.

5. Stir in the white wine, Cointreau and if preferred ice cubes.

6. Float the mint or lemon balm leaves on top and serve immediately

FRUIT AND VEGETABLE INDEX

Page references to preparation instructions are in **bold**. The other pages refer to actual recipes which include the particular fruit or vegetable.